FOREWORD

by Ben Pymer

From roughly 4000 BC, in and around the Tigris-Euphrates river system in modern day Iraq, the first cities of what is widely regarded as the oldest civilisation in the world, Mesopotamia, began to spring up. Before this time there were plenty of groups of humans who lived, worked and innovated together, but the people of Mesopotamia took this to a whole new level. Brought together by a common religion, they were a much larger group of more organised humans than their predecessors, with a social hierarchy, a written language and education system, moral codes, a mathematical system, the world's first banking system and an appreciation of the arts. They are also credited with numerous technological advances and some of the earliest use of logic. Whether or not you, as the reader, consider this first civilisation to be the first example of a society, it is undeniable that our modern day societies are significantly different to those of our ancient ancestors, even if there are certainly parallels to be drawn. There is only one way that these differences could have come about. Put simply, things changed. Whether these changes had a large impact on society, such as the industrial revolution or the founding of communism, or a smaller one, such as the switch from papyrus to paper, each generation has altered their society in some way. In his piece 'On Societal Change', Joshua Reid attempts to explore the different ways in which our societies do change and why these changes continue to come about. Reid also explores those areas of our societies that do not change, that which is fundamental to

Joshua Reid

the human condition.

ON SOCIETAL CHANGE

By Joshua Reid

Dear Jim & Carol,
I hope you enjoy reading
this. Thank you for all your
support.
God bless,
Josh

J Reid

CONTENTS

AN INTRODUCTION TO SOCIETAL CHANGE

By observing the history of society, and noting societal change, we, as philosophers, can begin to greater make sense of the world. By understanding societal change we can broaden our understanding of every aspect of philosophy and, therefore, develop and deduce more knowledge by which we can explore new ideas of the world.

To begin to understand societal change we must first outline and understand one basic truth, which I aim to make clear to you, my brothers and sisters, through my work.

There are only three types of change within society: material change, informational change and educational change.

We might define material changes as those of: advancement of technology; clothing trends and styles; the personalisation of the self; and the change of diet. Informational changes are simply the developments in mathematics and science. Whilst educational changes might be defined as: the development of language; the advancement of schooling; and the evolution of religion and politics.

All other fundamentals of society remain unchanged, including those that are behavioural, sexual/romantic and the eternal fight for moral perfection.

MATERIAL CHANGE

Material changes we understand through our *a posteriori* knowledge. As with all societal change, we can only grasp the true extent of this through developing our historical understanding. We, as philosophers, have a duty to be historians also, for where does our wisdom come from if not from that which has come before.

Material changes should be blindingly obvious, and often they are, but sometimes we forget to reflect and become ignorant to the evident truths around us, that materials have, and always will, change.

All humans have within them the basic desire for materials. Once we move past the simple animalistic desire to survive - which includes the need for 'essential materials' such as basic food, clothes and shelter - then we progress our human desires to 'excessive materials', this is where we find technological change, clothing trends, the personalisation of the self, and, to an extent, change of diet.

Of course, there are those of immense wilful strength whose lifestyle includes rejecting 'excessive materials', however, the majority are unable to do this, whether through circumstance or lack of strength, and so it comes to be: as long as there is human life, and society with it, there will also be material change.

INFORMATIONAL CHANGE

We know, through the efforts of our brothers and sisters of the past, that these changes fall within the *a priori* realm of our knowledge. We observe that as the first generation deduces *a*, so the next uses this to progress to the deduction of *b*, and the generation thereafter uses *b* to deduce *c* and so on.

It appears now that we have progressed beyond *z* into the unknown, where science is as much based on guesswork, theories and suggestions as it is fact. It seems now that science has evolved into a half-way house between *a priori* and *a posteriori* knowledge.

However, let us not be fooled into thinking this is the end of informational change, for as long as there is a new generation they will use the knowledge from the generation before to attempt to deduce the next natural evolution of knowledge. Whilst they may no longer be deducing *a*, *b*, or *c*, they may now be deducing *Alpha*, *Beta*, or *Gamma*.

EDUCATIONAL CHANGE

As with that of material change, we know of educational changes through our *a posteriori* knowledge.

We see, by assessing the languages of each country, that the gradual development of language is as inevitable as night and day. Whilst we cannot be infinitely certain of the sun rising and setting, we can be justified in our assumption that it will happen. Just as this is the case with night and day, so it is the same with language.

In regards to the progression of schooling, not only do we find gradual change in who is educated and how, we also find change in what they are educated in. We must understand schooling not only as within a conventional structure but also that of gender roles, industry, and any other skills or ideas that are learnt. By doing this we soon see the development in not only who has qualifications, how and in what, but also the development of industrial skills and other such professions or lifestyles that do not come with certificates, books and writings, but hold very much equal value. They also perhaps show us more clearly this development in education.

Like other listed changes, the development of religion and politics is one that should be blindingly obvious. That may be through the teachings of Muhammad (peace be upon him) quickly leading to Islam becoming the second largest religion, or the writings of Marx leading to varying socialist powers arising across the world (both in democratic socialism and communist dictatorships), or other such examples. Both politics and religion have, must, and always will play a crucial role in society, as we must keep control of our destinies through political struggle and give praise to the creator who gives us the ability to gain knowledge. It is inevitable that both religious and political thought will change as each individual is freethinking and desires their own understanding of God and politics. As it is part of our nature to think freely, the changes we see in religious and political thought will continue, just as with material change, so long as humanity and society continue.

OTHER FUNDAMENTALS

I n the initial outline the other are but a few examples of the other fundamentals of society, and whilst there are a large number to choose from, it is those examples that have been previously stated that shall be explored.

Human behaviour is the same today as it always has been, and I dare say, always will be. Since day one we have lied, cheated, caused harm and shown violent tendencies. Since day one we have also shown an ability to love, comfort, be patient and be kind. These simple human behaviours have never changed, they are innate within us, and are passed down from generation to generation. These behaviours need not be learnt, observed or habituated, they simply are part of our very being. The only time when we cease to live out these behaviours is in death - which we must learn to see as true life - for when we enter paradise our earthly, human behaviours will cease to be and we will dwell in an eternity of purity, where our being *imago dei* or having a God-like essence is exploded into an eternity of bright shining God-like essence. But in paradise society will cease to be, and thus this change cannot be considered in regard to societal change.

Sexual and romantic fundamentals also remain a constant, not just in the way of them existing, but also in the forms we see them. Promiscuity seems to be something which every generation blames the next generation of having too much of, but this is pure hypocrisy. Society has become no more or less promiscuous than it ever had been - there was as much promiscuity, homosexual activity and adultery in the days of Plato as there is now. We find the same conclusions when compared to Lot's exile from Sodom and Gomorrah, the letters of Paul (who was Saul), Henry VIII's rule of England, the Victorian era and the 1960s/70s. These things have not changed. Of course, there are those that abstain from all of this activity, however, unfortunately, as ever, these remain a small minority. Further, we find constants in those whose romantic and sexual life is spent with but one heterosexual partner, and also those who abstain from any sexual or romantic activity at all. Masturbation has existed since man found his genitals and woman found hers. Prostitution is 'the worlds oldest profession' and is very unlikely to ever disappear. It is clear for all to see that romantic and sexual fundamentals have been, and will remain, unchanged.

And finally onto the eternal fight for moral perfection. For since (wo)man first sinned we have battled for what we believe to be moral perfection, and to this day all but one have failed. The battle for moral good remains as alive today as it was yesterday and the day before. The moral battles are evidenced by the existence of religion and religious law since the first day. Even for the man or woman who prescribe to no religion the works of Kant, Bentham, Mill and any/every other moral philosopher influence their decision making. Every man, woman and child in their search for moral good pushes others towards prescribing to their moral good and, where this inevitably does not happen, conflict begins. All of these things are unchanged through the centuries.

All other fundamentals clearly remain unchanged when we read back through the history of society. And thus I proclaim that there are but three types of social change, and that is how it is likely to stay.

✳ ✳ ✳

Joshua Reid

* * *

OTHER PHILOSOPHICAL PIECES

Other pieces by the author

PHILOSOPHY - THE ART OF NOT KNOWING

P hilosophy is the friend of wisdom. But what is wisdom?

Wisdom put simply is knowing that you know nothing. The more you learn, the more you realise that you know nothing of the world, and the more you crave to know.

As philosophers we are tasked with the art of not knowing. A task we should take seriously, and yet enjoy. Relish in the art of not knowing and you will soon become well acquainted with wisdom.

"A fool thinks himself to be wise, but a wise man knows himself to be a fool." — William Shakespeare

* * *

WHAT IS THE THIRD WAY?

The third way seems, to me at least, to be the brainchild of a confused man.

The third way is like a person seeking God, but with no friend to guide them. The person tries many varying religions, but cannot settle on one, and so opts for living a life based on the aspects they like of all the religions they have tried. The person, after minimal contemplation, decides that their lifestyle works well, and becomes very proud. However, those who observe their lifestyle from the outside notice that it is somewhat dysfunctional; they see what the person, in their clouded partiality, cannot: that the resulting mishmash of all the ideas creates a mess of incompatibility.

The person tries to persuade others to join them in their new 'contemporary idealistic' lifestyle, and, for a time, some do. Though, after not too long the new 'followers' find themselves dissatisfied, and soon realise what the person has not: that living a life based in the 'best' of various differing religions leads to the 'worst' of all of them quickly showing their face.

Now, some time later, the person is walking around with a placard advertising their way of life as 'the future of humanity', but everyone else has long since moved on. Those that once tried the lifestyle are now disillusioned, with the memories of the disaster it caused still strong in their minds.

The third way has seemingly had its day. It was a brief 'new fad' in the history of U.K. politics. Put simply, and perhaps more explicitly, the third way was an incompatible mishmash of socialism and capitalism, that aimed to focus on the best of both, but inevitably the worst of both soon arose. It seemed to many as a good idea at the time, but left Britain waking up the morning after on the stone cold floor with a horrific hangover saying "Never again!".

❋ ❋ ❋

DO PHILOSOPHICAL ARGUMENTS FOR THE EXISTENCE OF GOD HAVE ANY EFFECT ON THE FAITH OF BELIEVERS?

F aith is a position of belief or understanding that does not rely on proof or evidence. From this definition it is clear that those of a position of faith do not need philosophical arguments for the existence of God in order for their faith in the existence of God to be real. However, that is not to say that faith cannot be affected by philosophical arguments. For many believers, their faith may be enhanced by proof or evidence in favour of their beliefs, and similarly it may be hindered by proof or evidence on the contrary. Despite this, there are still many believers for whom their faith cannot be altered by any proof, or a lack thereof.

It could be argued that people fall into one of two camps: 'fact driven people' or 'faith driven people'. 'Fact driven people', unsurprisingly, strive for facts, proved knowledge and things that are of an a posteriori nature. For 'faith driven people', their faith is enough. Philosophical arguments for the existence of God could be effective as a means of allowing 'fact driven people' to move into a faith position by offering a tangible or persuasive proof or evidence for the existence of God. Modern developments of the design argument, such as Darwin's Theory of Evolution, could provide the 'proof' or 'evidence' needed to 'fact driven people'. However, whether or not Darwin's Theory of Evolution could be classed as a proof is questionable. The mention of the word 'theory' suggests that Darwin's work is itself unproved, and is a piece of a posteriori knowledge if it is 'proved'. It may be evidence, however, as it shows a potential link between God and nature. 'Fact driven people' may instead look towards the Ontological Argument for proof or evidence. The Ontological Argument is a priori and therefore, if it is correct, it is a definitive proof. If correct it would be categorised in the same grouping of knowledge as that of mathematics, and so would be unquestionable. However, as of yet the Ontological Argument has not been found to be 100% correct and it is unsure if it ever will, as it relates to something which we cannot know of, according to Augustine's definition of God.

Furthermore, the philosophical arguments could be used by believers as a means of justifying their individual faith and beliefs. Those of a more conservative position may 'pick and mix' philosophical arguments that seem to prove their beliefs, for example, some may use Paley's watch analogy within the design argument to justify their creationist views. However, more liberal Christians may be inclined to take an overview of a wide range of philosophical arguments in order to justify their faith position.

Overall it seems that philosophical arguments for the existence of God can have varying effects on the faith of some believers. However, none are likely to completely destroy the faith of a believer. Further, there remain many believers for whom philosophical arguments have no effect on their position of faith. What is clear is that it is very much possible for one to hold a faith position and engage with philosophical arguments for the existence of God. The philosophical arguments for God were, after all, created by theologians of a faith position, and were created as much for those without faith to engage with as they were for those with faith to engage with.

✻ ✻ ✻

Joshua Reid

* * *

ABOUT THE AUTHOR

J oshua Reid is an active member of the Labour Party. He has studied the policies and decisions made by existing politicians, as well as their predecessors. Through the years his inspiration has come through works by Peter Hennessey, Harry Leslie Smith and Owen Jones, among many others.

Reid has spent time studying and writing on the relationship between Politics and Religion, especially the view that "Politics not only impacts upon religious groups but can also be impacted by religious groups as well".

In 2015, a mission trip to the Bethesda Life Centre in Goa gave him the chance to meet some of the poorest people in the world. As a result he developed a real understanding of the need for political and systemic change, giving him the drive and determination to make a difference through rebalancing the way wealth and basic necessities are distributed. Reid's election as Youth Officer for Woking Labour Party further developed him as a politician. After not too long he stood as the Labour and Co-operative candidate for Horsell in local elections.

The Communist Manifesto helped develop his views of global politics and personal beliefs. He found the concepts outlined by Marx and Engels intriguing and remained fascinated by the idea

Joshua Reid

of conflict between the bourgeoisie and the proletariats. Thus his political outlook and understanding of the world have developed and been shaped around the works of Marx.

As a Christian, Reid's philosophical and theological interests are mainly around Christian philosophy and theology. Notable inspirations of his include C.S. Lewis, Todd White, Ken Ham and Ray Comfort among many others.

A lot of Reid's early work focused around questions such as: why and how our spiritual beliefs affect our political and societal beliefs, why and how there is such variety in interpretation and belief within the Church, and why the western media and popular culture aim to be so secular and anti-religious when the vast majority of citizens are still religious.

Reid currently edits the website The Art Of Not Knowing, which is a hub for philosophy, theology and politics.

https://theartofnotknowingonline.wordpress.com/

ALSO AVAILABLE FROM THE AUTHOR

Other pieces from the author are available online at https://theartofnotknowingonline.word-press.com/

On Societal Change is also available to buy on Kindle.

Printed in Poland
by Amazon Fulfillment
Poland Sp. z o.o., Wrocław